T0153576

*To*_____

with best wishes
for your future happiness

from this day forward...

by Siggen Myhre

Translated by Bjarne Helland

with a Foreword by Donald Soper

LUTTERWORTH PRESS
London & Guildford

English translation
First published 1979

The Marriage Service (Series 3) is printed by permission of SPCK
Biblical quotations are from the Good News Bible (The Bible
Societies/Collins)
Illustrations are by Per Thoreson

FROM THIS DAY FORWARD first appeared as *Ekteskapet*
published by Instituttet for Kristen Oppseding, Oslo, 1975

ISBN 0 7188 2380 x

Printed in Great Britain by
Cox & Wyman Ltd,
London, Fakenham and Reading

CONTENTS

FOREWORD

The contents of this short book about marriage speak for themselves and it is no part of my responsibility to anticipate them. What I can do, and regard it as a privilege so to do, is to commend them.

From my own experience of conducting marriages, few brides or bridegrooms are at the moment of making their vows fully attentive to their meaning. The occasion is exacting, deeply emotional, and often contains elements of anxiety as well as of awe.

To the reader therefore perhaps the most valuable aspect of this book is not that it treads new ground. Indeed it is in a long succession of books on this theme. It is the way it links its propositions with the Bible in general and the Anglican marriage service in particular that I find particularly useful.

To ponder the words of scripture and liturgy contained in the marriage service quietly and intelligently before the actual ceremony is of great value on the wedding day and of greater value in the days that follow. This brief document offers such a valuable opportunity, and is particularly to be commended for the inclusion of some prayers which speak to the difficulties that the application of these marriage vows brings in its train.

Marriage is the most fundamental of all human relationships. To throw light on its importance, its difficulties and above all its benefits is very much worthwhile, especially at a time when the very institution of marriage is being denigrated, and its unique significance widely questioned. This author has no hesitation in offering the good news of Christian marriage as the peak of human experience. Hence the substance of the primer is good advice whereby those who enter the life of marriage may prove the good news which the ceremony that initiates it proclaims.

The style is simple but not simplistic—the reader is invited to understand the problems of living in holy wedlock. A man and a woman so linked together, whatever their physical, mental and spiritual attachment to each other, will surely find that accommodation to varying and differing personal characteristics of each partner is a continuous task which needs constant vigilance and tolerance.

To be forewarned about the upkeep of the marriage state is always more costly than the original outlay for the licence, but (to vary the metaphor) it is the preventive medicine which, if taken in time, can prevent the onset of those diseases like unfaithfulness, frigidity, mutual disrespect and downright hatred, which debilitate and all too often destroy married happiness. The reader will find a most perceptive and understanding approach to these infections.

Those contemplating marriage and reading this book will, I am persuaded, stand a better chance under God of fulfilling his divine purpose of which Christian marriage is an integral part.

DONALD SOPER

Dear newly-weds

Congratulations! The wedding ceremony may not last long, but it means a lot. During the ceremony it is difficult for a couple to remember all that is said, but here in this book you can find the wedding service with the promises you have made, together with some of the Bible verses that are often read and the prayers that are offered.

Here too are some thoughts on the subject of marriage.

Already you will have talked a lot about your marriage and how you intend to live in your new home. Maybe you have thought so much about it that you feel anything written here is superfluous. Nevertheless it may inspire both of you to continue the conversation about the new relationship into which you have just entered.

MARRIAGE

A Privilege and a Responsibility

A wedding day is a happy day. There is every reason for joy because marriage is God's gift. Now you have somebody to share everything with: the joys, the challenges and the difficulties.

The Bible says that a man and his wife shall be one flesh. This refers both to the sexual relationship in marriage and to the emotional relationship seen as a whole. Sadly it cannot always be taken for granted that marriage is marked by a good relationship and a feeling of togetherness. Some people even think that a successful marriage depends on chance and good luck, and it is certainly true that since we are all subject to the chances and changes of this life things sometimes happen which put a real strain on marriage and family life.

But the course of our life is not altogether left to chance. Life consists of many insignificant situations where we can choose what we do and what we say. All these apparently unimportant decisions mean something for our marriage and affect the way it turns out. Indeed, when they are added together they are so important that the responsibility for the marriage and how it develops might be said to rest primarily on ourselves.

Marriage therefore is both a gift and a task. We need to know what it entails and what is required of us, and then to go to it. If we do that, we shall find the good wishes on our wedding day will not be mere words. They will become a reality in the days and years to come.

Perhaps some readers will say that their expectations are not so high because they *had* to get married—they were expecting a baby! But even if they would have preferred a different start no one can take away from them the assurance that they have exactly the same chance of success as anyone else.

THE MEANING OF THE WEDDING CEREMONY

No Longer Alone

Until very recently few people would even have asked the question, 'Why get married?' Marriage was thought to be the all-important cornerstone of our society. The Bible says that it is not good for man to be alone and that men and women are created to live together in marriage. It is therefore the will of God that the desire for a close and permanent relationship with someone of the opposite sex should eventually lead to marriage.

Is the Wedding Ceremony Necessary?

Isn't love a private affair? Isn't it enough that we make our promises to one another?

We all have an in-born need to feel secure. Therefore we want to give security to the person we love. Real love shows itself where there is a willingness to accept both obligation to and responsibility for somebody else—without reservations. That feeling of security is strengthened by

15

the openness, the official ceremony and the binding agreement which the marriage service gives.

Faithfulness is one aspect of love. That's why the rules and regulations that govern marriage are not intended as coercive measures, but as a help in fulfilling responsibilities and safeguarding a loving relationship.

Moreover marriage concerns the coming generations, which is another reason for protecting it by legislation. The new home that is established usually concerns more than two people because marriage also has to do with children. The human triangle of mother, father and child is fundamental for the whole race. Primarily it is the parents who have the responsibility for the child, and the opportunity to give love, security and human contact.

16

HOW TO LIVE TOGETHER

'... Will you love her, comfort her, honour and protect her, and, forsaking all others, be faithful to her as long as you both shall live?'

'... Will you love him, comfort him, honour and protect him, and, forsaking all others, be faithful to him as long as you both shall live?'

Living Together Faithfully

The more familiar phrase is 'to live together after God's ordinance'. It means that we take the teaching of the Bible about love and let it be the foundation in our effort to love one another. There is one verse in the scriptures called the Golden Rule which clearly explains what love is: 'In everything do to others as you would that they should do to you.'

'To love and to cherish'

To love means primarily to show goodness. A person who loves will do everything he can to make life good and enjoyable for the one he loves.

In our everyday living love makes us say pleasing, encouraging words to one another, and do the

little things that we know will make our partner happy. At the same time we graciously accept the joys and encouraging words which they offer us. For most people this does not come naturally. It requires effort, ingenuity and determination.

Our partner is not our property. Even though marriage means having everything in common, it does not mean losing our own personality. We must accept one another as independent persons with their own abilities and attitudes. At the same time we must learn to show consideration for each other and be willing to change those things which make life difficult for our partner.

In marriage we also promise to honour each other. This does not mean that we shall be solemn and serious all the time but rather that in all our words and deeds we shall show respect, courtesy and even deference.

Those two small words *thank you* are of tremendous value. It should be as natural to use them when talking to our loved ones as it is when talking to strangers. Saying thank you shows both that we see what the other person is doing for us, and how we feel about it.

Our emotions vary according to our experience of joy and sorrow, and depend also on how tired or rested we are. Even though we would prefer to share everything and talk about everything in our marriage, there are times when it is better that we should keep quiet for the time being, and then talk later when it is easier. At the same time we must not be so 'considerate' that we never get to the point. That does not help either husband or wife.

There will, however, always be some tension points in a marriage, and it is wise therefore if we

consciously train ourselves to be tolerant so that we don't have to 'tip-toe' round each other too much.

All human beings need a sense of self-respect. In other words we need to know that what we do and what we are is of value to somebody else. Marriage is a golden opportunity to help our partner gain a sound self-respect by our attitude towards them, by our behaviour, and by showing consideration and thankfulness. Self-respect will also be built up when we show that we trust each other.

At times we all do things that make us feel awkward. Sometimes we buy something and later regret it, or we break something because we are careless. We even forget things and we lose things. On these occasions we all react differently. Some people make so many blunders that you could write a book about them, while others almost never do anything stupid. But where there is love there is also personal trust, which believes that the other partner is doing their best even if it doesn't always look like it.

'All that I have I share with you'

Openness and a willingness to talk things over are important conditions for a companionship which is to last a lifetime and to include all aspects of life. It might seem obvious, but it is not always so easy to agree on how to spend money or to use free time, while the division of responsibilities at home often leads to disagreements and discontent.

In any home both parents and children know that there are some topics it is wise to avoid. Talking about them creates an unpleasant atmosphere because solutions have not been found. But usually an attitude of keeping-quiet-if-at-all-possible is the easy way out. To avoid such problems it is usually best from the very beginning to agree to talk about everything, and especially about those things that are difficult.

No husband and wife can expect to agree on everything. There is nothing wrong with that. On the contrary disagreement can provide an opportunity for discussion and conversation which need not always lead to a quarrel. Respect for one another means coming to see that we have different opinions.

There are, however, some situations in which we do have to come to an agreement. We have to make a choice or give an answer. When for instance the house is to be decorated, we have to make many choices between different styles, different colours and various price ranges. When children ask if they can go to the cinema, they don't know where they are if mother says·yes and

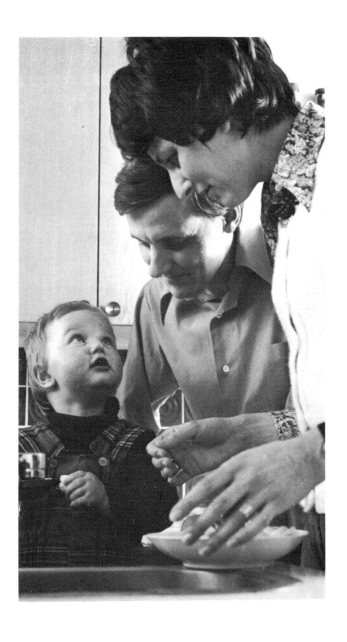

father says no! These and many other occasions are situations where we have to adjust so as to work out a solution together.

Every marriage undergoes change as the partners face new situations and challenges. Where there are children, different periods follow in quick succession: pregnancy, baby and child care, some hectic years with school children, maybe a stormy teenage period and then a more quiet time when husband and wife are on their own again. There will be times when parents and other older people in the family need particular care. New situations also arise when we change our job, move into a new home, experience a change in our financial situation, or find new friends and interests with duties and engagements outside the home.

Through all these different circumstances open and frank conversation need to be maintained, and conversation should include the future as far as it is possible to foresee it. New tasks and problems are much easier to solve when discussed openly and tackled together.

Silence is not always golden—in marriage it can develop into a deadly poison. About the worst and most damaging thing that can happen in a home is when one partner clams up in an ice-cold silence and so more or less tyrannizes the other.

'For better for worse'

Marriage vows are realistic and related to life. Because not all life is a bed of roses, as they say, marriage vows expressly include *all* days—days of illness and days of difficulty. Some difficulties husband and wife confront together. At other times events may relate more specifically to one than to the other, such as responsibility for parents or problems at work. Within marriage, however, between two people who love each other, there can be nothing bad or difficult which exists only for one of them. Everything concerns them both and everything can be shared.

Sometimes in the marriage service this verse of scripture is read: 'Bear one another's burdens and so fulfil the law of Christ.'

Most married couples fairly soon find out a few of each other's faults and weaknesses. In such a close relationship they simply cannot be concealed. In times of difficulty this means there is always a temptation to expose the other partner to anyone who is willing to listen. This is the time when the person who *really* loves will keep quiet and even try to cover up their partner's weaknesses.

It is of course quite a different situation when we are going through extreme difficulties and have to seek professional guidance from someone we can trust like a clergyman, marriage guidance counsellor or social worker. Then the bond of loyalty is not broken because we are not setting out to expose our partner. On the contrary, we are trying to restore a relationship that may be on the point of collapse.

'In sickness and in health . . . till death us do part'

Can we really promise to love anybody for the whole of our life?

We all change as time goes by. What we think of as falling in love might be a sweet infatuation. We all know that our feelings change. So it would be impossible to give a promise to be in love with the same person throughout all our life, even though some seem to manage it.

But love is much more than 'falling in love'. Real love has something to do with our willpower: the will to fulfil the obligations and accept the responsibilities on the bad days as well as on the good days. The initial thrill may fade, but love is different and that is why it *is* possible to enter into marriage for life.

Faithfulness

The will to be faithful is the foundation of marriage.

Even after we are married we shall still go on meeting people of the opposite sex who are charming and attractive. The temptation to flirt and to be unfaithful will still be there, particularly if there are difficulties in the marriage. Some people flirt to seek comfort in someone who 'understands'.

28

Others do it just to convince themselves that they can still attract interest and attention. Some flirt with the express purpose of making their partner jealous, and so preventing them from feeling too secure. 'After all there may be others. . .' But every kind of flirtation is a serious offence against a marriage partner.

Marriage is a relationship of trust. It can only be satisfactory when both partners seek to live in such a way that they deserve to be trusted.

Is Real Love Beyond Our Capability?

Once we think about what it means to love some-body with everything we've got for the whole of our life, we soon discover how difficult it is. We don't have unlimited resources of good will or 'loving capacity'. The result is that when we compare what we really are with what we like to think we are, we may begin to lose heart.

There are two ways of overcoming this discouragement. One way is to give up and to say to ourselves that it is too much to expect. We can never live up to such a standard anyway. Better to take life as it comes, without giving it too much thought, and then hope for the best.

The other way is to keep the ideal in front of us but then say, 'Being the sort of person I am, it looks as if I shall need to practise hard if this is going to work out ... but I'll certainly try.'

None of us will ever get so far that we no longer need forbearance and forgiveness. That's why we have to work hard so as to develop a forbearing disposition, a will to forgive what is wrong and a readiness to see what is positive and good.

When we need forgiveness, it is always difficult to ask for it in words. It is much easier to let the problem slip by without mentioning it. But if we can muster enough courage to do it then our relationship becomes better and more open. It is a humbling experience and therefore it will also make us more careful in the future.

Difficulty in a marriage is not the greatest disaster. What is worse is the lack of a will to forgive or to seek forgiveness.

Physical Joys

Sexual relationships in marriage are not just for the sake of producing children. They are of great value in themselves. For both husband and wife they are a very special way of showing tenderness, goodness and care, and of expressing devotion and joy in each other—of being one. To caress each other and to have bodily contact is a way of continually renewing our love throughout our marriage.

People today are very outspoken about sex, yet there are still many married couples who never talk together about how they feel on this most intimate of subjects. They feel inhibited. They see sexual relationships as something 'necessary'—something that just happens to be part of the deal—rather than something good and enriching in itself.

Success in sex presupposes an emotional and spiritual relationship, for sexual relationships cannot be seen as an isolated part of marriage. Only when sex is seen as part of a greater whole can it give the richest experience of love.

Yet the part of married life which is so wonderful and rich in possibilities can easily be disappointing to the point of becoming both uncouth and problematic. This happens if coercion, demand, or lack of consideration is given a chance to get in and destroy the relationship. It also happens if certain conditions are laid down for intercourse: 'I will . . . if . . .' something or other.

The fine and delicate feelings which surround the sexual relationship are also hurt by coarse and dirty remarks. Pornography almost forced on us

by magazines and newspapers may do a lot of damage to our relationship.

Many other situations can make sex difficult. It may be the fear of becoming pregnant when you don't want to. Tiredness, over-exertion and cramped living quarters also can have adverse effects. Many people are not aware that it takes surplus energy to make this side of married life successful.

Some people have difficulty because they lack the necessary knowledge. We need to know how men and women react sexually—each in his or her particular way. Others, because they lack purely practical information which would make relationships easier.

It is also natural that it takes time to adjust and get to know each other. Sexual relationships vary through the years in intensity and rate of success. But when both partners in a marriage keep this in mind and are open about it even the difficulties experienced can become positive stepping-stones, and true love will grow.

There are many books on the subject, as well as specialized help from marriage guidance counsellors, clergy or doctors. They are all there to help.

What about Money?

Disagreement about the use of money is very often the reason married couples seek help. Experience shows that it is very easy to get into conflict over this, especially where both partners are responsible for home and finance according to their abilities and job possibilities.

We live in a rapidly changing society. We cannot say that one particular family pattern is the right one. Each family must work things out for itself, as the situation requires. At the same time we must never forget that the children's need for security and for ample contact with both parents is so important and fundamental that it can never be ignored. Lately we have become particularly aware of how very important it is for a child to have a close and almost continual contact with its mother during the first three years.

Once we have given proper attention to the needs of children then we can begin to think about how the work inside and outside the home should be divided. For many this will change as the children grow up. Yet the marriage may suffer if the workload becomes so heavy that personal contact becomes superficial.

Traditionally, in the West women have worked mainly in the home. Nowadays, as more and more women also work outside the home, it becomes obvious that the work and duties in the home must be shared if the woman is not to have two occupations. Helping each other with the shopping, washing and other practical chores also builds up a feeling of unity in the family.

This is apparent to some degree even when the wife stays at home. Sharing the chores upgrades the effort made by wives, and makes the relationship easier in that it gives an understanding of what things cost and what housework entails.

When there are children, the job of a wife in the home is just as demanding as the work others have in their particular professions. At some stages it is *very demanding* because the children need attention and care at all hours of the day and night. A wife who is at home does not have the advantage of a change of scenery, meeting new people and then leaving her place of work and being free to do what she wants.

Most wives have an allocation of money for housekeeping. Housekeeping money is not a gift, but a right. The amount must be in proportion to the family income, which a wife should know. And apart from real financial difficulty it should always be adequate for basic needs.

Where a wife has her own income there is no reason why this should not also go into the common purse. It is not something she can keep for herself, any more than the husband can keep his income to himself. Where the income is sufficient, however, it is a good thing for both husband and wife to have some money they can use at their own discretion.

Talking about these things with openness, trust and a willingness to change is the foundation for solving some of the economic problems of marriage, and so preventing conflicts which otherwise might damage a relationship.

In talking about money we should always include other important questions such as: how comfortably do we really want to live? Do we buy things and clothes according to what others have, or just according to our needs in our particular situation?

TO CREATE A HOME

What Really Makes a Home?

A house has a structure that everybody can see: table, chairs, beds and kitchen utensils, walls, ceilings and all the personal things—few or many. The structure is necessary. It is of great value if we are to make it as convenient as possible for the family at all times.

Just as important as the structure is something that we cannot see: the atmosphere, the mood, the prevailing spirit in the home.

A home should be *a good place to be in* for all who live there, a place where we feel secure and where we are accepted as we are. At our place of work we are often expected 'to play a role', to behave in a particular manner. At home we should be spared from such expectations and be able to be our natural selves in front of each other. So that all who live in a home may experience it as a good and safe place we need to attend to a few practical points.

Space, for example. If there are children, the way different members of the family relax varies so much that they cannot always use the same room: parents may like to rest, read or watch television, while the children may want to play or listen to music. When we plan our homes, therefore, we have to think not only about suitable furniture but also about the way we use the different rooms in the available space.

Both parents and children are individual human beings with abilities and needs of their own. Sometimes it happens that different members of the family go the same way, and find common duties and activities inside or outside the home. But just as often it happens that the interests are different. This too can give joy and freshness to the family providing it does not lead to sharp and agonizing opposition between its members.

The Home—Also For Others

Growing as people is more than developing abilities and gifts for our own enjoyment. Many people have discovered that the most enjoyable experience of all is doing something for somebody else, and this is always a possibility both for individuals and for families.

If we have a home, we have a great gift. We can share it with others by keeping an open home for relatives, friends, neighbours, friends of the children, and not least for older people.

Many different sorts of home study group are fast developing. Some are simply gatherings to discuss a common interest and a discussion and light refreshments provide an opportunity for contact and fellowship. Groups and clubs for the children can also be started in homes.

We need to think about how we really want to use our home. When we have settled that we will be able to decide how to furnish it.

Joy and Cheerfulness

Every married couple and every family have experiences that are theirs and theirs alone. This creates a particular 'language', a common joy in a family, provided we understand how to let these experiences create joy and pleasure later on.

A family needs to let trifles remain trifles. Home is a place where we can drop all pretence and formality, because these only create stiffness and boredom. Their loss will affect neither our personality nor our authority as far as the children are concerned.

To Help Each Other Spiritually

During the marriage service the minister prays for the wedding couple. This is because the congregation believes that God, who is a living God, who hears prayers and who has an infinitely great compassion for each human being, continues to care for us when through marriage we enter a new era of life—a relationship which is according to God's will and purpose.

Dare We Pray Together?

Some people are very reluctant to talk about the spiritual side of life. Maybe they feel a yearning for it, but uncertainty and apprehension make them afraid to discuss it—even when they are husband and wife. This is sad. Many of the difficulties that all married couples meet have a much greater chance of being solved if a couple can learn to pray together.

This is not something only for the very religious, but for everyone. A verse of scripture sometimes read during the marriage ceremony says: 'Have no anxiety about anything, but in everything by prayer and supplication with thanksgiving let your requests be made unto God.'

It sometimes seems as if there is a great wall to be broken down before two people can start praying together. They are not used to it and feel embarrassed and ill at ease. Some, however, have started by having a time of prayer together at the end of the day. They felt a need to give thanks, and in this way something started that became a good habit throughout life.

What Shall We Pray About?

We can thank God and share all our worries with him just as simply and straightforwardly as we would do with a good friend.

When the disciples asked Jesus to teach them how to pray he taught them the Lord's prayer.

Very many people find help simply by repeating the Lord's prayer; others make up their own prayers.

In the Lord's prayer we ask: 'Forgive us our trespasses.' This is asking God for forgiveness. When we ask God for forgiveness together, it then becomes easier to ask forgiveness of each other, for we have then admitted together that we stand in need of it. It is then not only easier but absolutely necessary to forgive each other, for the prayer goes on: 'Forgive us our trespasses as we forgive those who trespass against us.' This prayer is therefore always important in the daily life in the home.

To Help Each Other in the Faith

Not all who start praying together continue. Tiredness, the demands of every day, or maybe even a 'tiff' bring it to an end. Then suddenly something which both really wanted to do from the beginning stops.

Faith in God needs nourishment if it is to exist and grow. It increases and grows in strength when we read and hear the scriptures. This is why we need to go to church, read the Bible and pray.

In some marriages only one of the partners wants to do this. Since God never forces anyone to do anything, no more do we have the right to force one another in any way. To seek God either in private prayer or by going to church is something which should always be done voluntarily. Equally, on the other hand, we have no right to hinder a partner who wishes to live in faith, even though that faith may not mean anything to us.

When something as basic as faith is understood differently by husband and wife, difficulties easily arise. It often happens that one partner comes to faith while the other still remains far from it. As in all other situations in marriage, it is very important to talk about these things and try to reach clear understandings on such matters as, for instance, how to spend Sunday.

Many have the idea that they have to become very religious and pious before they dare to pray or start going to church. It is not true. Everyone stands in constant need of God's forgiveness and help. Faith is turning to God and praying for forgiveness and help, believing that he will give it.

DEVOTION IN THE HOME

We have included in this book some prayers for those who want to start praying together. In the beginning it may not be so easy to formulate prayers in your own words. You may become self-conscious. But the prayer is no less genuine if you pray with words that others have written.

Besides these prayers, you will probably want to pray about other things, such as people you know who are ill and others who suffer in different ways. There may also be current events in the country or in the world which you want to place before God. You can do this in a few informal words and mention the names of those whom you particularly want to pray for.

To read together from the Bible may not be so easy if you do not have a plan. One suggestion is to start in the New Testament and read a chapter a day. Reading from the Psalms will also prove a great source of inspiration. Bible-reading plans can usually be obtained from a Christian bookshop.

We have nevertheless added a few readings from the Bible in the hope that these passages may start you off and give you the inspiration to continue reading together. Alternatively you could use books of daily devotions. Your choice of books will depend on whether there are children in the family.

It is always best to have a regular time of prayer together in the morning. In this way you start the day by placing it in God's hands. It then also comes naturally to thank God together at the end of the day. But the pattern differs from family to family. In each home you have to find the right time and occasion. The most important thing is that we seek it and make time for it. It will not start by itself. Nobody has time unless he makes time, which requires both willpower and effort, because other things can so easily appear to be more important.

THE MARRIAGE SERVICE

The bride and bridegroom stand before the priest, and the priest says,

We have come together in the presence of God, to witness the marriage of N and N, to ask his blessing on them and to share in their joy. Our Lord Jesus Christ was himself a guest at a wedding in Cana of Galilee, and through his Spirit he is with us now.

The Scriptures teach us that marriage is a gift of God in creation and a means of his grace, a holy mystery in which man and woman become one flesh. It is God's purpose that, as husband and wife give themselves to each other in love throughout their lives, they shall be united in that love as Christ is united with his Church.

Marriage is given, that husband and wife may comfort and help each other, living faithfully together in need and in plenty, in sorrow and in joy. It is given, that with delight and tenderness they may know each other in love, and, through the joy of their bodily union, may strengthen the union of their hearts and lives. It is given, that they may have children and be

51

blessed in caring for them and bringing them up in accordance with God's will, to his praise and glory.

In marriage husband and wife belong to one another, and they begin a new life together in the community. It is a way of life that all should honour; and it must not be undertaken carelessly, lightly, or selfishly, but reverently, responsibly, and after serious thought.

This is the way of life, created and hallowed by God, that N and N are now to begin. They will each give their consent to the other; they will join hands and exchange solemn vows, and in token of this they will give and receive a ring.

Therefore, on this their wedding day we pray with them, that, strengthened and guided by God, they may fulfil his purpose for the whole of their earthly life together.

The priest says to the congregation,

But first I am required to ask anyone present who knows a reason why these persons may not lawfully marry, to declare it now.

The priest says to the couple,

And if either of you knows a reason why you may not lawfully marry, you must declare it now: for the vows you are about to take are to be made in the name of God, who is judge of all and who knows all the secrets of our hearts.

Stand

The priest says to the bridegroom,

> N, will you take N to be your wife? Will you love her, comfort her, honour and protect her, and, forsaking all others, be faithful to her as long as you both shall live?

He answers,

> I will.

The priest says to the bride,

> N, will you take N to be your husband? Will you love him, comfort him, honour and protect him, and, forsaking all others, be faithful to him as long as you both shall live?

She answers,

> I will.

Either A:

The priest may receive the bride from the hands of her father.
The bride and bridegroom face each other. The bridegroom takes the bride's right hand in his, and says,

> I, N, take you, N,
> to be my wife,
> to have and to hold
> from this day forward;

for better, for worse,
for richer, for poorer,
in sickness and in health,
to love and to cherish,
till death us do part,
according to God's holy law;
and this is my solemn vow.

They loose hands.
The bride takes the bridegroom's right hand in hers, and
says,

I, N, take you, N,
to be my husband,
to have and to hold
from this day forward;
for better, for worse,
for richer, for poorer,
in sickness and in health,
to love and to cherish,
till death us do part,
according to God's holy law;
and this is my solemn vow.

They loose hands.

Or B:

The priest may receive the bride from the hands of her
father.
The bride and bridegroom face each other. The bride-
groom takes the bride's right hand in his, and says,

I, N, take you, N,
to be my wife,
to have and to hold
from this day forward;

for better, for worse,
for richer, for poorer,
in sickness and in health,
to love, cherish, and worship,
till death us do part,
according to God's holy law;
and this is my solemn vow.

They loose hands.
The bride takes the bridegroom's right hand in hers, and
says,

I, N, take you, N,
to be my husband,
to have and to hold
from this day forward;
for better, for worse,
for richer, for poorer,
in sickness and in health,
to love, cherish, and obey,
till death us do part,
according to God's holy law;
and this is my solemn vow.

They loose hands.

The priest receives the ring(s). He says,

Heavenly Father, by your blessing, let *this*
ring be to N and N a symbol of unending
love and faithfulness, to remind them of
the vow and covenant which they have
made this day; through Jesus Christ our
Lord.

All   Amen.

The bridegroom places the ring on the fourth finger of the bride's left hand, and holding it there, says,

> I give you this ring
> as a sign of our marriage.
> With my body I honour you,
> all that I am I give to you,
> and all that I have I share with you,
> within the love of God,
> Father, Son, and Holy Spirit.

If only one ring is used, before they loose hands the bride says,

> I receive this ring
> as a sign of our marriage.
> With my body I honour you,
> all that I am I give to you,
> and all that I have I share with you,
> within the love of God,
> Father, Son, and Holy Spirit.

If rings are exchanged, they loose hands and the bride places a ring on the fourth finger of the bridegroom's left hand, and holding it there, says,

> I give you this ring
> as a sign of our marriage.
> With my body I honour you,
> all that I am I give to you,
> and all that I have I share with you,
> within the love of God,
> Father, Son, and Holy Spirit.

56

The priest addresses the people.

In the presence of God, and before this congregation, *N* and *N* have given their consent and made their marriage vows to each other. They have declared their marriage by the joining of hands and by the giving and receiving of a ring. I therefore proclaim that they are husband and wife.

The priest joins their right hands together and says,

That which God has joined together, let not man divide.

The congregation remain standing. The husband and wife kneel, and the priest blesses them.

God the Father,
God the Son,
God the Holy Spirit,
bless, preserve, and keep you;
the Lord mercifully grant you the
   riches of his grace,
that you may please him both in body
   and soul,
and, living together in faith and love,
may receive the blessings of eternal life.

All   Amen.

Kneel

The husband and wife kneel before the holy table.

Priest Almighty God,
you send your Holy Spirit
to be the life and light of all your people:
open the hearts of these your children to
the riches of his grace,
that they may bring forth the fruit of the
Spirit
in love and joy and peace;
through Jesus Christ our Lord.

All   Amen.

Either or both of these prayers are said

Heavenly Father, maker of all things, you
enable us to share in your work of creation.
Bless this couple in the gift and care of
children, that their home may be a place of
love, security, and truth, and their children grow up to know and love you in
your Son Jesus Christ our Lord.

All   Amen.

Lord and Saviour Jesus Christ,
who shared at Nazareth the life of an
earthly home:
reign in the home of these your servants as
Lord and King;
give them grace to minister to others as
you have ministered to men;
and grant that by deed and word

they may be witnesses of your saving love
to those amongst whom they live;
for the sake of your holy Name.

All **Amen.**

Priest As our Saviour has taught us,
so we pray:

All **Our Father in heaven,**
hallowed be your Name,
your kingdom come,
your will be done,
on earth as in heaven,
Give us today our daily bread.
Forgive us our sins
as we forgive those who sin against us.
Do not bring us to the time of trial
but deliver us from evil.
For the kingdom, the power, and the glory
are yours
now and for ever.   Amen.

The priest blesses the couple and the congregation saying,

God the Holy Trinity make you strong in
faith and love, defend you on every side,
and guide you in truth and peace; and the
blessing of God Almighty, the Father, the
Son, and the Holy Spirit, be among you
and remain with you always.

All **Amen.**

SOME PRAYERS

Thanksgiving and Prayer for the Marriage

Thank you, Heavenly Father, because you have created the two of us to live together in marriage.

Lord, may our marriage become a joy and a blessing, but because sometimes marriages end in unhappiness and despair, we would ask you always to be near to us with your help and power.

Strengthen our love for each other.

Help us to bring each other joy.

Give us the will to understand and accept each other.

Give us time to pray together, and to commit everything into your hands.

Help us to please you by being good to each other, and to the people around us, for Jesus' sake.

Amen.

We Expect a Child

Gracious Father, thank you for the great miracle that has happened; for a new life has begun.

Lord, use the time in waiting to prepare us for the big task and responsibility that follow.

In our joy we still feel so uncertain and insecure.

Help us to give the little human being loving care and security, and a sound and right upbringing.

Thank you for loving our child.

Amen.

We Expect a Child who was not Wanted

Heavenly Father, you see and you know everything. You know now just how we feel.

We struggle and have difficulties, and this pregnancy is not our choosing.

Lord God, help us so that our despair may be turned to expectation. Let it happen, Lord, so we can receive our child with joy and thanksgiving.

Help us to solve the practical problems that make this situation difficult for us, and give us all we need to become good parents, so that we can give our child security and warmth and true guidance in life.

Amen.

Prayer when Marriage becomes Difficult

Heavenly Father, we confess before you that our marriage is far from what we hoped it would be when we started.

You have heard our words, and you know our thoughts.

Help each of us see our own faults.

Help us to ask each other for forgiveness without reservation and save us from trying to justify ourselves.

Give us a deeper understanding of each other, help us to listen and to be willing to fit in with one another.

Lord God, forgive us that we have offended you by not earnestly seeking to keep the peace and understanding between us.

Help us to find our lost unity again and to maintain it, for Jesus' sake.
Amen.

Intercession for our Loved Ones and our Home

Thank you Father for all our loved ones whom you have given to us.

For our parents, brothers and sisters and all who are near and dear to us.

Please keep them from all evil and show us what good things we can do for them.

Help us to maintain a good relationship so that no envy, bitterness or other bad feelings may come between us.

Amen

Lord, we ask for your blessing upon our home.

Let love prevail here, so that it may be a joy to those who visit us and a source of strength for those who live here.
Amen.

SOME WORDS FROM THE BIBLE

God's Word in our Home

Love the Lord your God with all your heart, with all your soul, and with all your strength. Never forget these commands that I am giving you today. Teach them to your children. Repeat them when you are at home and when you are away, when you are resting and when you are working.

Deuteronomy 6:5–7

Love Is . . .

Love is patient and kind; it is not jealous or conceited or proud; love is not ill-mannered or selfish or irritable; love does not keep a record of wrongs; love is not happy with evil, but is happy with the truth. Love never gives up; and its faith, hope, and patience never fail.

1 Corinthians 13:4–7

Great or Small?

At that time the disciples came to Jesus, asking, 'Who is the greatest in the kingdom of heaven?' So Jesus called a child, made him stand in front of them, and said, 'I assure you that unless you change and become like children, you will never enter the kingdom of heaven. The greatest in the kingdom of heaven is the one who humbles himself and becomes like this child.'

Matthew 18:1–4

Our Example

After Jesus had washed his disciples' feet, he put his outer garment back on and returned to his place at the table. 'Do you understand what I have just done to you?' he asked. 'You call me teacher and Lord, and it is right that you do so, because that is what I am. I, your Lord and teacher, have just washed your feet. You, then, should wash one another's feet. I have set an example for you, so that you will do just what I have done for you. I am telling you the truth: no slave is greater than his master, and no messenger is greater than the one who sent him. Now that you know this truth, how happy you will be if you put it into practice!'

John 13:12–17